The Waterman/Harewood Piano Series

Piano for Pleasure
Book 2

easy classics – solo and duet

selected and edited by
Fanny Waterman and Marion Harewood

Faber Music Limited
London

Piano for Pleasure follows *Piano Progress* (by the same authors) in providing a graded sequence of pieces by master composers from Bach to Bartók.

Here is an enjoyable, varied repertoire for the pianist who has mastered a basic technique.

Alongside the solo pieces there are duets, which will provide a welcome opportunity for players to enjoy making music with others.

Contents

SOLOS

DUETS

This collection © 1989 by Faber Music Ltd
First published in 1989 by Faber Music Ltd
3 Queen Square London WC1N 3AU
Music drawn by Sambo Music Engraving Co
Cover designed by John Bury
Printed in England
All rights reserved
Halstan & Co. Ltd., Amersham, Bucks.

The Prince of Denmark's March

Jeremiah Clarke
(1673-1707)

Bourrée
from BWV 820

Johann Sebastian Bach
(1685-1750)

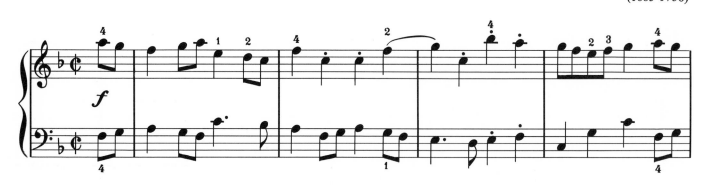

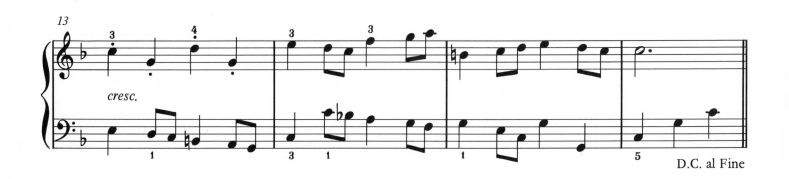

Allegro I and II

I

Johann Wilhelm Hässler
(1747-1822)

II

Repeat Allegro I

Rondo

K.15hh

Wolfgang Amadeus Mozart
(1756-1791)

D.C. al Fine

Romanze

from Sonatina in G, Anh. 5/1

Ludwig van Beethoven
(1770-1827)

Minuet

Ludwig van Beethoven
(1770-1827)

Allegretto

Carl Czerny
(1791-1857)

Album Leaf

Robert Schumann
(1810-1856)

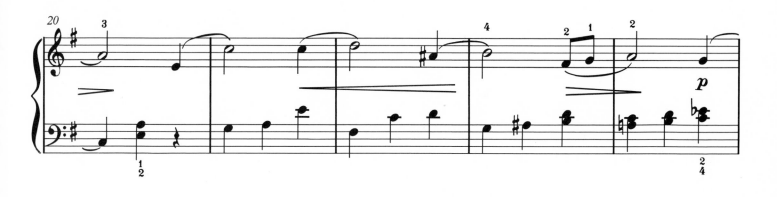

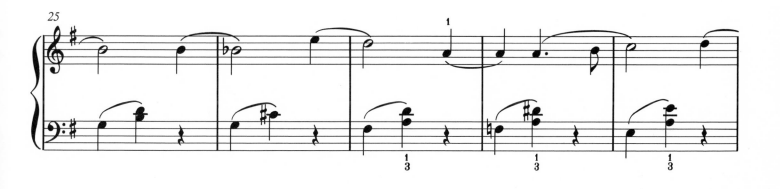

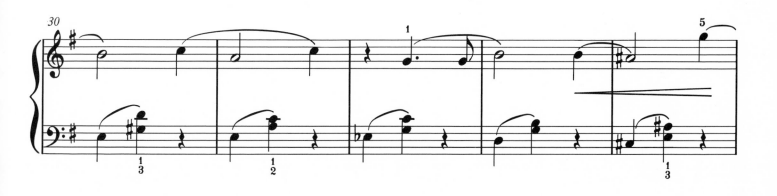

German Dance

Franz Schubert
(1797-1828)

Mazurka

Op.155 No.2

Theodor Oesten
(1813-1870)

Polka

Cornelius Gurlitt
(1820-1901)

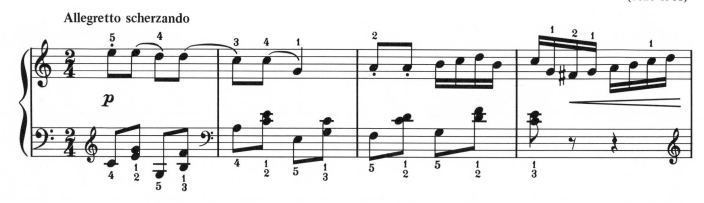

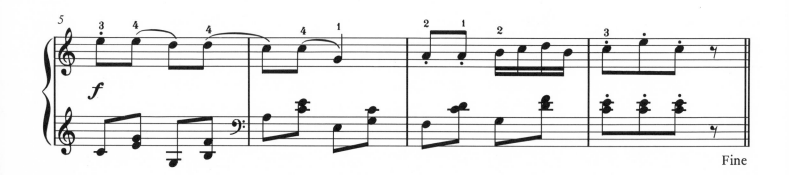

Fine

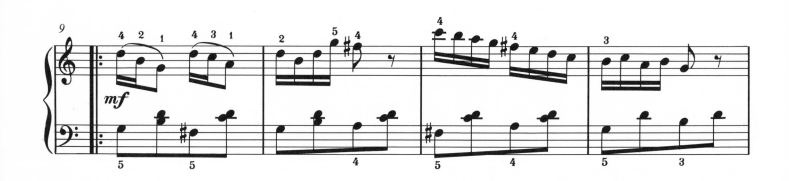

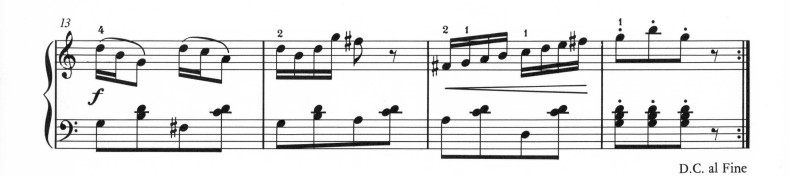

D.C. al Fine

Slow Waltz

Cornelius Gurlitt
(1820-1901)

Gavotte

from Serenade I, Op.183 No.1

Carl Reinecke
(1824-1910)

Fine

The Sick Doll

Peter Ilyich Tchaikovsky
(1840-1893)

Children's Polka

A. Jilinskis

March

P. Hadgiev

Song of Twilight

Yoshinao Nakada
(b. 1923)

Tranquillo (♩ = 60)

Mazurka

Op.68 No.3

SECONDO

Frederic Chopin
(1810-1849)

Mazurka
Op.68 No.3

PRIMO

Frederic Chopin
(1810-1849)

Allegro ma non troppo

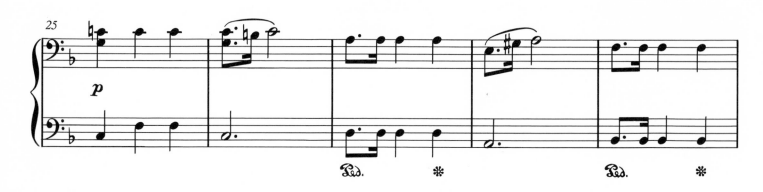

Mimi en Marquise

SECONDO

Déodat de Séverac
(1873-1921)

Fine

poco rit.

D.C. al Fine

Mimi en Marquise

PRIMO

Déodat de Séverac
(1873-1921)

D.C. al Fine

The Fairground

SECONDO

J.E. Hummel
(19th century)

D.S. 𝄋 al Fine

The Fairground

PRIMO

J.E. Hummel
(19th century)

D.S. 𝄋 al Fine